GHOST LIGHT

Desi Moreno-Penson

I0140313

BROADWAY PLAY PUBLISHING INC
New York
www.broadwayplaypublishing.com
info@broadwayplaypublishing.com

GHOST LIGHT

© Copyright 2011 by Desi Moreno-Penson

Cover image by Alan Buttar
I S B N: 978-0-88145-506-9
First printing: October 2011
Book design: Marie Donovan
Page make-up: Adobe Indesign
Typeface: Palatino
Printed and bound in the U S A

GHOST LIGHT was first produced as a co-production by The Immediate Theater Company (Producing Artistic Director, Jose Zayas) and Monarch Theater, (Artistic Director, Jennifer Ortega) at 59E59 Theater, (President & Artistic Director, Elysabeth Kleinhans; Executive Producer, Peter Tear) in New York City from 14-31 October 2009. The cast and creative contributors were:

NATALIE ....Kate Benson
BRIAN..Bryant Mason
MARTY ....Hugh Sinclair

Director..Jose Zayas
Scenic designer...Jason Simms
Lighting designer...Evan Purcell
Stage manager..Toby Ring Thelin
Sound designer..David M Lawson

CHARACTERS & SETTING

BRIAN, *30s-early 40s, successful actor: charismatic, outwardly amiable, sense of entitlement, smug, slightly passive and complacent.*

NATALIE, *30s-early 40s years old, struggling playwright/ actress: easily angered, acerbic yet sensual, charming in a deeply neurotic, fixated way, cynical and insecure.*

MARTY, *30s-early 40s years old, security guard at motel, also a playwright, deceptively affable, manic, effortlessly excitable, can also easily lose his temper.*

Time & place: A rundown motel room. Doesn't really matter what it 'looks' like, as long as it appears as though it's seen better days. It would help if the audience could actually see the bathroom door; however, the door that opens into the room can be off-stage. Also, the light bulb should be in a prominent, central location of the room as well as the mirror. In all honesty, the mirror should face the audience, so during the production, they're forced to see their own faces.

Playwright's note: Although the play appears to be written as either a straight drama and/or a "ghost story", I've always seen it more as a "black comedy", and I would encourage the director and cast to keep this in mind during rehearsals.

Now the image in the mirror was the foreigner, and I was the mirror. I stared at that mysterious, terrifying stranger before me, and it seemed to me appalling to be left alone with him.
–*Rainer Maria Rilke*

Only liars prosper.
–*Anonymous*

(Setting: motel room)

(Sounds of buzzing flies blend into the sounds of crushing machinery, back to a low, pulsating hum which cues a lone, hanging light bulb stuttering on and off in darkness. Finally, it stays on to illuminate a slightly tacky motel room, but not necessarily a dirty one; a large, cloudy, gray-splattered window nearest to the bed, matching nightstands with small lamps on each stand, neither of the lamps are on, an aged clock radio sits on one of the nightstands, a small, broken-down vanity, a writing desk, and a small wardrobe off to the side with an ages-old, antennaed television on top. Next to the wardrobe, is a small table with a hotplate, two freshly-cleaned coffee cups with saucers, and a few, tightly-wrapped plastic cups. Amidst all this, we see NATALIE and BRIAN. They must have just walked in since they're both still wearing their coats. They stand across from each other, both of them nervous, expectant. A beat.)

BRIAN: Okay.

NATALIE: Yeah.

BRIAN: Yeah.

NATALIE: Okay.

BRIAN: Can I get you something?

NATALIE: Like what?

BRIAN: *(Looking around)* I don't know...water?

NATALIE: Do you have water?

BRIAN: In my bag.

NATALIE: Oh.

BRIAN: Would you like some?

NATALIE: I don't know...maybe...later...

BRIAN: Okay.

NATALIE: Thanks.

BRIAN: No problem.

NATALIE: *(Not looking up)* There's a mirror on the ceiling.

BRIAN: I know. I noticed it when we walked in.

NATALIE: It's ridiculous.

BRIAN: Try not to think about it.

NATALIE: It doesn't bother you?

BRIAN: I'm ignoring it.

NATALIE: *(Looking towards the window)* There are flies outside the window.

BRIAN: In this place, I'd be surprised if there weren't.

NATALIE: No, they're not inside. They're outside. I bet there's a nest or something. *(Puts her hands and face up against the glass)* They're loud.

BRIAN: We can keep the window closed

NATALIE: You've been here before?

(As NATALIE speaks, the light bulb stutters above them and goes out for a brief moment, and then comes back on again.)

BRIAN: No. But I was surprised when you suggested it. I've only heard about the place. From a friend.

(Cell phone rings. Neither of them makes an attempt to answer it.)

NATALIE: Is he married, too?

BRIAN: Who?

NATALIE: Your friend.

BRIAN: He was...he's divorced now.

NATALIE: Oh.

BRIAN: Yeah. *(Looking around room)* This place doesn't seem very popular, does it?

NATALIE: I've heard it is. *(Smile)* For hookers, anyway.

BRIAN: *(Chuckles, begins to relax, and nods)*Definitely for hookers, yes.

NATALIE: *(Laughs)* I guess that makes you my 'john,' right?

BRIAN: *(Self-conscious chuckle)* No, not at all.

NATALIE: *(Laughs also)* Or maybe my 'pimp,' right?

BRIAN: Yeah, maybe. *(Playing with her)* Get over here, bitch.

NATALIE: Oh. Funny.

BRIAN: *(Still playing)* Look at me when I'm talking to you, bitch. Where's my damn money at?

NATALIE: That's good.

BRIAN: Would you like that? 'Cause we can play. *(Taking off his coat)*We can pretend. Like that.

NATALIE: *(Removes her coat)* Sure. Role-playing.

BRIAN: Yeah.

NATALIE: Like what you were just doing.

BRIAN: Yeah.

NATALIE: You're an actor.

BRIAN: You're a playwright.

(A beat. NATALIE notices a large, plastic ashtray; she takes out a pack of cigarettes from her backpack, pulls a cigarette out and lights it, inhaling deeply. BRIAN sees this.)

BRIAN: I don't think you can smoke in here.

NATALIE: *(Pointing)* There's an ashtray on the nightstand.

BRIAN: There is? *(Goes to look)*

NATALIE: If it's there, it must be okay to smoke, right?

BRIAN: I wouldn't chance it if I were you.

NATALIE: Then they shouldn't put ashtrays in all the rooms.

BRIAN: It may not be in all the rooms. It may just be in this room.

NATALIE: Why would it be in this room and not in any of the others?

BRIAN: I don't know. It could just be there for show.

NATALIE: For "show"? *(Laughs)* Why would they put an ashtray in here if they don't want any ashes in it? Doesn't that seem strange to you?

BRIAN: Actually, people don't just use ashtrays for smoking. I'm in hotel rooms all the time, and I use it to keep my loose change, my watch, my wedding band—

(Cell phone rings. BRIAN pulls it out, it's his phone. He looks to see who's calling, and then hastily puts it away. NATALIE sees this. An awkward beat)

BRIAN: *(Notices her staring at him; sheepish)* Sorry about that.

(NATALIE puts the cigarette out and throws it away.)

NATALIE: Not a problem. See? It's gone. All gone.

(Another awkward moment. BRIAN reaches over to touch her.)

BRIAN: I've always had a little crush on you, Nat.

NATALIE: *(Chuckle)* I want to giggle like a teenager when you say that.

BRIAN: *(Smile)* That's good.

NATALIE: I never expected to see you at that reading...!

BRIAN: I know! I didn't think I'd see you at all—I thought you were still in...

NATALIE: *(Hastily)* Oh, I left there a while ago.

BRIAN: For good? Or...are you expected to go back...?

NATALIE: Why would I want to go back?

BRIAN: *(Slight unease)* Well...you know...do you ever have to go back in from time to time, just to get re-checked...just for safety's sake? You know...just to make sure you're feeling 'okay' about everything?

NATALIE: I feel fine. But I do go back for my refills, if that's what you mean.

BRIAN: *(A little worriedly)* Oh. Are you...on something?

NATALIE: *(Smile)* You mean right now?

BRIAN: Well—

NATALIE: *(Reassuring; laughs)* It's okay...

(Light bulb stutters again. A short beat)

NATALIE: You were really good in Killer Saints of Avenue B.

BRIAN: Thank you.

NATALIE: No. I mean it. I think it was some of your best work.

BRIAN: Spencer wrote the part with me in mind, so he knew I could play it.

NATALIE: *(Simply)* I hate Spencer.

BRIAN: Why?

NATALIE: 'Cause he's a successful playwright.

BRIAN: We've all got to start somewhere.

NATALIE: What's he working on now?

BRIAN: Well, he's been busy doing the L A thing; taking meetings and all that. But he's back in town now; I think he just wants to become a bigger name so he can do plays on Broadway. He's got discipline issues when it comes to his writing.

NATALIE: Meaning what?

BRIAN: He doesn't like to write.

NATALIE: *(Bitter snort)* A hugely successful playwright who doesn't enjoy writing...Jesus, this fucking business—

BRIAN: You shouldn't hate people for being more successful than you.

NATALIE: Why not?

BRIAN: It messes with your karma...

(NATALIE laughs.)

BRIAN: I'm not kidding. The universe sees you're not happy—
And when it comes time for something great to happen for you, the universe will go, "No, I don't think so... that person is too spiteful.
Too hateful.
Too full of envy
Too hungry.
Too bad.
Screw her."
And then you'll end up losing a great opportunity Because you've got a bad attitude.

NATALIE: Wow...Someone has spent way too much time on the west coast.

BRIAN: Don't you agree?

NATALIE: No. You're being simplistic.

BRIAN: How so?

NATALIE: I use my hatred as a motivating force for my art.

BRIAN: *(Shaking his head)* No. Hatred can't be used as a motivating tool.

NATALIE: Bullshit.

BRIAN: You're trying to tell me that hate motivates you?

NATALIE: Yes, that's what I'm telling you.

BRIAN: Hating people makes you feel good?

NATALIE: No. I'm saying that it motivates my art. Since when does work make you feel good?

BRIAN: Have you any idea how bad that sounds?

NATALIE: Why? Why is that bad? The best work comes out of rage, and passion, and fury—

BRIAN: But that's so negative...

NATALIE: What, to feel empowered?

BRIAN: *(Emphatic)* Hatred cannot make you feel empowered!

NATALIE: *(Fiercely)* Sometimes the more wound up I feel, the more determined I am to get my work out there and show those motherfuckers what I can do.

BRIAN: Yeah...and that's pretty warped.

(An uneasy moment between BRIAN and NATALIE.)

NATALIE: This will go bad.

BRIAN: It won't.

NATALIE: Maybe we shouldn't do this.

BRIAN: We should. I think we should.

NATALIE: We should have an affair.

BRIAN: *(Shakes his head)* No.

NATALIE: No?

BRIAN: Not an affair. It won't be an affair.
(*After a beat*) Affairs get messy.
An affair means
We stake emotional claims on each other. That's not
going to work for me.
If I have to be out of town
On a gig for eight months
I can't have someone calling my cell every five seconds
going, "Hey! Where the fuck are you?"

NATALIE: Okay.

BRIAN: This will be an arrangement.

NATALIE: A secret arrangement, right?

BRIAN: Yes. We're a secret.

NATALIE: A big secret.

BRIAN: My wife can never know.

NATALIE: 'Cause it's a secret.

BRIAN: I value our friendship.

NATALIE: Our secret friendship.

BRIAN: But I can't lose my marriage over this.

NATALIE: Not over a secret.

BRIAN: And I don't want to be the cause of any kind of
break-up between you and your husband, you know?

NATALIE: Of course not.

BRIAN: This is about fun. Having fun. That's it...just fun
and friendship.

NATALIE: And what happens when it stops being fun?

BRIAN: Then we go back to being friends.

NATALIE: And if we can't go back to being friends?

BRIAN: *(Teasingly, sexy; short beat)* I don't know, baby. Then maybe we'll disappear. Would you like that? Would you like to disappear with me?

NATALIE: *(Responding)* Maybe.

(BRIAN and NATALIE kiss. A hint of foreplay; the energy between them is suddenly ardent, intense.)

BRIAN: *(Almost a whisper)* Take off your clothes.

NATALIE: You first—

BRIAN: Come on...do a little dance for me...let me see that ass.

NATALIE: *(Pulling away from him)* You probably have enough women dancing for your pleasure out in L A.

BRIAN: Not really. I'm not that attractive.

NATALIE: *(Laughs)* That doesn't matter! Don't be so pathetic. Once you're successful, everything comes... That's it. It just COMES—like a big, happy, hairy, pussy puppy. You know that. We all want that.

BRIAN: Well, I also care about doing good work.

NATALIE: *(Scornful)* Oh, fuck you. Fuck you, Brian... FUCK YOU. "Oh, I care about doing good work," that's about as cliché as the fucking mirror above us.

BRIAN: *(A little smug)* That's not true. You can be a successful actor and still keep your integrity. Success in this business is all about the combination of hard work, confidence, and humility—

NATALIE: This is not a fucking interview, alright? I'm not asking for an autographed picture once I suck your dick.

BRIAN: *(A short beat)* You...um...you're kind of a bitch, aren't you, Nat?

(A short beat.)

NATALIE: I'm sorry, okay? That was wrong.

BRIAN: No. It's cool.

NATALIE: No, I was out of line, and I'm sorry—

BRIAN: It's perfectly alright.

NATALIE: I know I'm neurotic and insecure—

BRIAN: Listen, it's okay...

NATALIE: And I have trouble censoring what I say, sometimes, and...

BRIAN: No, listen, it's okay. It's okay. I can take it. I kinda like it. You challenge me. That's good.

NATALIE: *(A beat)* It's good?

BRIAN: Yeah. You're volatile. It's hot.

NATALIE: *(Flirty; a beat)* Yeah? *(Another beat)* You like volatile women?

BRIAN: *(Responding)* I like volatile women very much, yes.

NATALIE: *(A beat)* I punched my director once.

BRIAN: You did?

NATALIE: Yeah.

BRIAN: Wow.

NATALIE: Yeah.

BRIAN: That's intense.

NATALIE: Well, I'm not proud of it...of course...

BRIAN: No, of course not.

NATALIE: But...I...I was really upset at the time.

BRIAN: I can imagine... *(Starting to unbutton her shirt; sexily)*...I can be pretty volatile myself, you know.

NATALIE: You? You always seem so level-headed.

BRIAN: I'm a good actor.

(NATALIE *laughs again.* BRIAN *leads her over to the bed and slowly pushes her down upon it, continuing to kiss her and covering her body with his own. He rubs himself against her until she begins to moan softly in her throat.*)

BRIAN: Do you feel that?

NATALIE: Yes.

BRIAN: Do you like it?

NATALIE: Yes.

(BRIAN *erotically rubs himself against her.*)

BRIAN: How about now? You like what I'm doing now?

(BRIAN *props* NATALIE's *body up, with her back to him. He places his hand between her legs and begins to caress her crotch. With his other hand, he takes hold of one of one of her breasts.*)

NATALIE: Do you remember when we were sitting in the cab on the way over here...? Do you remember what we talked about?

BRIAN: No.

NATALIE: We didn't.
We just sat there.
I kept looking out the window, at all those passing streets.
And all I could hear was the engine buzzing against my spine
All I could feel was the glass window up against my fingers.

BRIAN: I want to taste you.

NATALIE: Open your pants.

BRIAN: Oh? I thought I was pathetic.

NATALIE: You are, but you're a celebrity. And I want to fuck a celebrity. Even a pathetic one.

BRIAN: Okay.

(BRIAN *and* NATALIE *begin to have sex. He turns on the clock radio. Music begins to play. She lowers her head and simulates giving him a blow job. The buzzing from the flies escalates in sound. A small illumination emanates down towards them from the ceiling mirror—like a soft, radiant shine; it envelops them both in its glow. Although he does not notice it, she reacts as though she can. As her head turns upwards towards the light, it begins to appear that she sees something. And whatever it may be, it frightens her. He immediately notices her moving away from him. The room goes back to "normal". A dramatic beat.*)

BRIAN: What happened? Why'd you stop?

NATALIE: I'm sorry. It's just the mirror. I hate that fucking mirror—

BRIAN: I told you to forget about it.

NATALIE: I'm sorry…I looked up and…

BRIAN: Come on—

NATALIE: I saw another face…

BRIAN: (*This stops him; he shuts off the music, turning back towards her*) Excuse me?

NATALIE: I looked up…I looked up…! And for a moment, I saw another face over mine. And then it was gone.

BRIAN: What are you talking about?

NATALIE: (*Indicating the mirror*) It wasn't me. Up there. That's what I'm saying. I looked up, and instead of seeing my face, I saw a different face. I saw a different woman.

BRIAN: What the hell is this, Nat? Huh? Did you change your mind?

NATALIE: I didn't say that.

BRIAN: No. You didn't have to… *(He's offended; he rises, fixes his clothing)* I think I'm starting to get the gist here—

NATALIE: I'm telling you the truth.

BRIAN: Look…if you're feeling weird about this, that's okay…just don't play these games with me, alright? I'm a big boy, I can take the rejection. It's fine. We don't have to do this. We can go.

NATALIE: I'm sorry.

BRIAN: Let's just go.

(NATALIE stares at BRIAN for a moment. She then gets up out of the bed and sexily moves towards him.)

NATALIE: Okay. Let's disappear together.

BRIAN: What?

NATALIE: You said we could disappear together.

BRIAN: *(Awkward laugh)* Well—

NATALIE: That's what you said, isn't it?

BRIAN: I don't think we're there yet.

NATALIE: No? Alright then… rescue me.

BRIAN: Rescue you?

NATALIE: Yeah. You're a big strapping guy. Why don't you rescue me?

BRIAN: From what?

NATALIE: From my own obscurity.

BRIAN: You're not obscure.

NATALIE: Everyone says so.

BRIAN: *(Smile)* If you think people are saying you're obscure, then you're probably not.

NATALIE: I think my existence as an artist is… ambiguous at best. I'm like a mushroom—

BRIAN: *(Amused by her)* Are you?

NATALIE: Yeah. I'm kept in the dark and fed shit.

BRIAN: *(Chuckle)* Very clever. But you know...women can't be rescued. Not anymore.

NATALIE: Yes they can.

BRIAN: *(Shaking his head)* No, I happen to have it on very good authority that it's impossible to rescue a woman.

NATALIE: And why is that?

BRIAN: They don't appreciate it. Oh, they might still secretly relish the idea, but they'll fight you tooth and nail, especially someone like you.

NATALIE: Oh, I'm a sweetheart—

BRIAN: Like hell!

(BRIAN and NATALIE laugh. Short beat)

NATALIE: Maybe I want you to rescue me... professionally.

BRIAN: Meaning what?

NATALIE: Meaning you help me produce my next play.

BRIAN: I don't produce independently any longer. I'm just an actor now.

NATALIE: No, no, I know that. But you know other producers. You know...other producers in your company.

BRIAN: *(Suddenly guarded)* Yeah, but those guys don't like being approached—

NATALIE: But they don't mind being approached by someone they know, someone they trust—

BRIAN: It's not that easy.

NATALIE: It's always been easy for you, baby...

BRIAN: Unless producers know that a certain playwright has real potential, they're just not interested. Besides in New York, potential is bullshit. You can't sell tickets on potential. So, if a playwright doesn't even have that, what's the point?

NATALIE: *(Short beat)* Are you saying I don't have potential as a playwright?

(Another beat. BRIAN suddenly realizes he might be in trouble.)

BRIAN: No! I mean...no, of course not. I've read your work, I've seen it—

NATALIE: Then what are you saying?

BRIAN: I'm saying it's about more than just handing a producer a script, alright? It's a very complicated process. It's tricky. It's about encouraging the producer to take a chance. Reassuring the producer that he's not wasting his time. Wasting his money. That the playwright is actually WORTH THE READ. And you can't say that about every writer. It's not always about who-you-know—

NATALIE: *(Rising anger)* No, that's right. It's not. It's not always about who-you-know...Sometimes it's about who-you-don't-know...and how do you figure out a way to finally get to know who-you-don't-fucking-know, when you're dealing with a business that's all about WHO-YOU-KNOW!

BRIAN: *(Sensing trouble)* Calm down—

NATALIE: And you...YOU know everybody!

BRIAN: It's not my responsibility—

NATALIE: And you have never ONCE made an effort to introduce me to Spencer...!

BRIAN: You never asked me to introduce you.

NATALIE: Oh bullshit!

BRIAN: You never asked…!

NATALIE: Why are you here?

BRIAN: What?

NATALIE: Why are you here with me?

BRIAN: I want to be with you.

NATALIE: Why?

BRIAN: Nat—come on…

NATALIE: I'm not a successful artist. I'm not part of your circle.

BRIAN: That has nothing to do with it.

NATALIE: I think it has everything to do with it.

BRIAN: No. I wanted you.

NATALIE: Why?

BRIAN: Jesus, Nat—

NATALIE: Why would you want to fuck regret when you've already passed it?

BRIAN: That's not how I see you.

NATALIE: Why would you want to have anything to do with me at all?

BRIAN: Because I can—

NATALIE: You can?

BRIAN: I can.

NATALIE: Meaning what?

BRIAN: You're not a risk for me.

NATALIE: What does that mean?

BRIAN: It means you're not a risk.

NATALIE: But how am I (not a risk)?

BRIAN: (Overlapping) You're not a risk…!

You're not any kind of a risk. Okay?
You're safe.
You're not real.
You don't even exist.
(A beat) NO ONE I know professionally would ever
believe I'd have an affair with you.

NATALIE: *(After a beat)* You just feel guilty.

BRIAN: Come on…

NATALIE: No, you do. You do! You cheat on your
wife, and now you feel guilty. You have a career
you'll protect no matter who gets hurt, and so you feel
guilty—

BRIAN: Fuck you.

NATALIE: You are completely flooded with GUILT.
You think you're a nice guy, but you are all rotted out
inside with the guilt.

BRIAN: I am a nice guy.

NATALIE: You've got the guilt leaking out of your
pores.

BRIAN: *(Rising anger)* I'm a terrific person—

NATALIE: You're like some great, big, fucking water
balloon, but instead of being filled with water, you're
filled with GUILT.

BRIAN: I can be one charming motherfucker when I
want, alright?
People like me
They like working with me
They like drinking with me.
Playing poker…they say to my face, "Gee, Brian—
you're such a cool guy," and then they go to my wife
and tell her she's lucky
LUCKY to have a husband who's not 'out there' doing
what every other married man is doing

Looking for other women
Looking for strange.
Just looking to get away with all kinds of shit.

NATALIE: So, you're a liar.

BRIAN: I have issues with fidelity.

NATALIE: You're a hypocrite.

BRIAN: *(He's had it)* I'M AN ARTIST! And if I said I'd produce one of your fucking plays you'd grab your cell phone so goddamn fast and call your husband so he could come down and watch you SUCK MY COCK.

(A sudden, sharp knock on the door. BRIAN and NATALIE are both startled. A beat.)

BRIAN: What the fuck...?

NATALIE: Shit.

BRIAN: Relax. Nobody knows we're here. We're not here.

NATALIE: What do we do?

BRIAN: It's going to be okay. We're not here. We were never here.

(Another forceful knock.)

NATALIE: *(To herself)* Fuck... Fuck.

BRIAN: It's okay. I'll take care of this. Just relax.

(Another loud knock. NATALIE is now even more frantic.)

NATALIE: *(Yell)* Motherfucker... Go away...!

BRIAN: *(To her)* Stop it...I told you, I got this... *(At the door)* Yeah? Who is it?

MARTY: *(From behind the door)* Found your wallet, sir.

BRIAN: Excuse me?

MARTY: Your wallet.

(BRIAN *opens the door. Enter* MARTY. *He is dressed as a security officer. He hands* BRIAN *a wallet.*)

MARTY: Is this your wallet, sir?

BRIAN: *(Looking at it)* No... No...I don't think so. It's not.

MARTY: *(Coming in)* Are you sure? I found it out in the hallway. Then I heard voices coming from in here. They told me at the front desk that you were in this room. It's my job, you see. *(Indicating his jacket; proudly)* I take care of security here at the motel.

(Another awkward beat.)

BRIAN: What's your name?

MARTY: *(He's looking around the room)* Hmm?

BRIAN: Your name?

MARTY: Oh...Marty. *(Another beat. He smiles at them, reassuringly.)* It's okay...I'm not a thief. Or a murderer. You're both safe. I handle security here at the motel... *(Indicates his jacket again)*

BRIAN: Oh no, no...I wasn't thinking anything like that.

MARTY: It looks like you were.

BRIAN: No. Not at all. *(Holding out a few dollars towards him)* Here you go.

MARTY: *(Looking at it, suspicious)* What's this?

BRIAN: It's a tip.

MARTY: *(Shaking his head)* Oh, I can't do that, sir. I can't. I mean, we're not allowed.

BRIAN: It's not a big deal.

MARTY: Oh, I understand that, sir...Tips are meant for people who do nice things for those who can reward them. I get it. We should all be applauded for our efforts. After all, life is hard. I understand completely...

it's a nice system. But security personnel are just not allowed to take tips. Management sucks cock...

BRIAN: What?

MARTY: *(Without missing a beat)* Management is strict.

BRIAN: Oh. But I want to show my appreciation.

MARTY: It's not your wallet.

BRIAN: Excuse me?

MARTY: I know it's not your wallet. It's my wallet.

BRIAN: What are you talking about?

MARTY: *(Taking a moment; deep breath)* I had to see who's in here.

BRIAN: *(Suspiciously)* Why?

MARTY: Because you shouldn't be in here. Nobody should be in here. But the person who's working at the Front Desk today is new, so it's possible he didn't know. Or he forgot.

BRIAN: I'm sorry...I don't understand...?

MARTY: There have been reports. About this room.

NATALIE: *(Alert)* What kind?

MARTY: Reports of disturbances, ma'am. Ghosts.

(A beat. Both BRIAN and NATALIE stare at MARTY, dumbfounded. NATALIE emits a nervous chuckle, but BRIAN remains silent. Suddenly, MARTY begins to giggle.)

BRIAN: What is it?

MARTY: I'm sorry, but...I know you, don't I? I do, don't I? *(To NATALIE)* He's a celebrity, isn't he? I mean, he is, right? *(No response from either BRIAN or NATALIE. He continues.)* Sure. I recognize you from that TV show...

BRIAN: *(Attempt to be gracious; shakes his hand)* Yeah. That's me.

MARTY: Sure. Sure...Once you recognize somebody that means they're a celebrity, right? I mean, you are, right? A celebrity. *(Short beat)* I usually have no respect for actors; if they're not famous then what purpose do they really serve?

NATALIE: What's your name again?

MARTY: Marty.

NATALIE: That's cute. You look like a Marty. So, what's Marty short for?

MARTY: I think it's just Marty. Before she died, my mom saw this dumb movie, and that's how she found out about the name...she always liked it.

NATALIE: Oh, of course. Marty. Ernest Borgnine.

MARTY: Who?

NATALIE: Brian, tell him who Ernest Borgnine is.

(The light bulb stutters above them and goes out for a brief moment, and then comes back on again. MARTY notices this.)

MARTY: *(Pointing to it)* Has this been happening since you've been here?

BRIAN: What?

MARTY: The light bulb going on and off like that--?

BRIAN: *(Shrugs)* Yeah?

MARTY: No, I'm talking about faulty wiring...This is how fires get started.

BRIAN: *(To NATALIE)* I think we should leave.

MARTY: Oh no, please—let me make this right, okay? I'll go back downstairs and see if there's another room available—

BRIAN: That won't be necessary...

MARTY: No, no, look...it's the least I can do after intruding on the two of you like this. I'll be back, I promise. I'll be right back. *(He exits.)*

BRIAN: *(To* NATALIE*)* Come on, get dressed.

NATALIE: *(Looks out the window; a short beat)* I bet the ghost is someone who died out there.

BRIAN: *(Starting to dress)* Yeah?

NATALIE: Yeah. After the accident.

BRIAN: That was a while ago.

NATALIE: I bet they talk about it. I bet they see apparitions of people dressed in business suits walking around every day...just wandering the streets as if in a complete daze. I mean, there's no way of letting them know they're dead, you know? *(After a beat.)* When I was a kid, I used to see my grandfather. Even after he'd been dead for years.

BRIAN: You're kidding.

NATALIE: *(As she dresses)* I'd get up in the middle of the night to go pee and I'd have to walk through the dining room in my parents' house. And I'd see my grandfather...I'd see him... Just sitting there, at the dining room table, like he always did, drinking his Lipton Tea and smiling at me. Sometimes he would look like he was about to say something, but whenever I'd see him, every time...I would get really cold and my heart would feel like it was going to shoot through my chest and then sweat would pour through my skin like ice-water. All I could do was run back into my bed and hide under the covers like a baby.
My parents never believed me. They thought I was lying just to get attention. I was told to stop. My mother even stopped buying Lipton Tea. So, in junior high, I used to hold Ouija Board sessions in

my bedroom with all my girlfriends. And we'd try to
contact my Gaga—that's the name I used to call him.
Something always came through on the board. But I'd
heard that it's only bad spirits that come and talk to
you on the Ouija. So…just to test it, I asked about his
head.

BRIAN: His head?

NATALIE: *(A beat)* He was decapitated…I mean that's
how he died. He was in a car accident…

BRIAN: He lost his head in the accident?

NATALIE: *(Nodding)* Right at the impact, it came clean
off his body. And it was never found. He had to be
buried without it. I needed to know what happened.
Where the head was…why it was never found. That
way I'd prove to my folks that I hadn't lied to them,
that I really did see my Gaga in the dining room,
drinking his tea. But every time I'd ask the question,
the board would stay silent. *(Short beat)* Except for one
thing…it kept spelling out the word "mill". That's it.
Just that one word…Mill.
It didn't make any sense. It didn't mean anything.
After a while, I stopped asking the question and I
stopped playing with the damn board. I thought it
was bullshit. I started thinking that maybe I had lied
about seeing him—maybe I'd imagined it, and I never
saw anything at all. Then a few months later, my
parents were contacted by the police; they found my
Gaga's head—immediately after the collision with his
car, the head was thrown off the freeway and rolled
down a long hill, right into the courtyard of this old,
abandoned textile mill.
(Short beat) It was real. What I'd seen…what had been
said to me on the Ouija Board. Suddenly, it was all real.

BRIAN: But when you saw him in the dining room, he
still had his head on, right?

NATALIE: *(Suddenly sheepish)* Well, yeah...I mean; yeah he did...but...um...

BRIAN: *(After a short pause)* What? Did he have his head on or not?

NATALIE: *(Having difficulty)* Well…when I'd see him there, drinking his tea...yes, he'd have his head on... but...I could tell...I could tell that his head...his head would be... *(She begins nodding her head side to side)*... bobbing up and down on his shoulders…

(BRIAN laughs.)

NATALIE: ...And he'd keep putting his hand up to HOLD his head *(Shows him)*...as though he were trying to balance the thing and just...just keep it up there, you know? What? What is so damn funny?

BRIAN: *(Still laughing)* Your grandpa's a bobble-head!

NATALIE: I was just a kid, Brian, okay? It was pretty creepy—

BRIAN: *(Forces himself to stop laughing)* Okay, I'm sorry.

NATALIE: *(Offended)* Do you do that to your wife?

BRIAN: What?

NATALIE: Do you make fun of her like that when she tells you something personal about herself?

BRIAN: I wasn't making fun of you—

NATALIE: Really? What do you call it?

BRIAN: You have to admit, it's a silly story.

NATALIE: And your wife doesn't tell silly stories?

BRIAN: *(A beat)* Don't talk about my wife.

NATALIE: Why? Is she perfect?

BRIAN: Natalie—

NATALIE: Is she an intellectual?

BRIAN: I'm not going to talk about her.

NATALIE: Is that why you don't fuck her?

BRIAN: I'm not going to talk about her. I am not going to talk about MY FUCKING WIFE! Jesus. What's wrong with you?

NATALIE: I don't like being made fun of.

BRIAN: I wasn't doing that.

NATALIE: I'm not less than her, you know.

BRIAN: I never said you were.

NATALIE: But when you tell me I can't talk about her it makes me feel like I'm less than her. And I'm not. I'm not less than her. I'm just as good as anybody. I'm just as good as your wife.

BRIAN: Have you noticed my wife scratches her arm a lot when she talks to you?

NATALIE: *(Short beat)* So?

BRIAN: She says that sometimes talking to you makes her feel so uncomfortable she breaks out in a rash. *(A beat)* It's true; she told me. She says you make her feel itchy. You make a *lot* of people feel itchy.

(Cell phone rings. They both react physically to the sound. A beat. BRIAN reaches out for her, but she physically moves away. Although she's 'acting tough' we can see she's been hurt by what he's said.)

NATALIE: Answer your damn phone.

(BRIAN pulls out his cell phone and answers it.)

BRIAN: Yeah. Hey Spence…

(BRIAN disappears into the bathroom, but he leaves the door slightly ajar behind him. NATALIE looks after him for a moment. Suddenly, there is a loud knock at the door, which momentarily startles her. She walks over and opens the door; it's MARTY again.)

MARTY: I asked the front desk about moving you guys to another room, but there's none available right now. *(Notices that* BRIAN *is not there; his voice changes)* Where is he?

NATALIE: In the bathroom.

MARTY: Oh.

*(*MARTY *and* NATALIE *stare at one another. This is a suddenly strange and awkward moment. He walks over to the bathroom, and points to the door. She nods.)*

NATALIE: Yes, he's in there. *(A beat)* There's an ashtray here. Can I use it?

MARTY: Why would it be there if you couldn't use it?

*(*NATALIE *eagerly grabs her bag, and pulls out a pack of cigarettes. Placing herself up against the wall, she offers one to* MARTY, *who promptly reaches over and takes one. She hands him her lighter and he lights both their cigarettes, handing the lighter back to her. A beat as they enjoy their smokes for a moment, like two sneaky and devious little children. They smile at each other, but they remain completely silent. The light bulb continues to stutter but does not go out. Sounds of a toilet flushing and* BRIAN *re-enters the room. Upon seeing him,* MARTY *immediately puts out his cigarette. However,* NATALIE *continues smoking hers. She observes* BRIAN *witheringly.)*

NATALIE: *(Sarcastic)* Everything okay?

BRIAN: *(To* NATALIE; *disapproving)* Why are you smoking?

NATALIE: *(Indicating* MARTY) He said I could.

MARTY: Actually, ma'am, there's no smoking in any of the rooms.

NATALIE: *(To* MARTY; *seemingly shocked)* Are you kidding?

MARTY: The ashtray's just there for show.

BRIAN: Exactly!

NATALIE: *(To* MARTY; *short beat)* You're a fucking liar.

BRIAN: Natalie...!

NATALIE: A fucking liar!

MARTY: No, ma'am...you asked to use the ashtray...and I was polite and said you could, but I handle security here at the motel so I have to uphold the law. And the law of the State of New York says there's no smoking in any of the rooms.

NATALIE: *(Puts the cigarette out; offended)* But you said I could smoke...you stood right there and you smoked one of my cigarettes!

MARTY: *(To* BRIAN*)* You never told me who Ernest Borgnine was—

(Ignoring him, BRIAN *takes the ashtray, he notices the cigarette butts.)*

BRIAN: *(Disapproving; he empties the ashtray)* Jesus, Nat... you smoked these while I was in the bathroom?

NATALIE: Brian, he smokes! He smoked one of them! The other butt is his...!

MARTY: Sir, if she had persisted with the smoking, the front desk would have no choice but to charge you with a twenty-five hundred dollar fine.

BRIAN: *(To* MARTY*)* Yeah, fuck that. Get this out of here.

MARTY: *(To* BRIAN*)* Who's Ernest Borgnine?

*(*BRIAN *holds the ashtray out towards* MARTY, *but* NATALIE *jumps up from the bed and quickly grabs it out of his hand.)*

NATALIE: No. It's my ashtray; let him get his own.

BRIAN: Natalie, come on—

NATALIE: No!

BRIAN: Technically, it's my ashtray...I'm the one paying for the room, okay?

MARTY: I'm sorry, sir—but the ashtray is the property of the motel management.

BRIAN: Just give him the ashtray, Nat, alright?

NATALIE: No, I don't think so.

BRIAN: (*Almost to himself*) I don't believe this—

MARTY: Who's Ernest Borgnine?

BRIAN: (*To MARTY; an eruption*) An actor! He's an actor! Okay? He was in the film Marty! He won the Academy Award for his role in Marty!

(*The light bulb stutters. This time there is a sudden, static sound accompanying it that we have not heard before. However, it doesn't appear that BRIAN and NATALIE hear this except for MARTY. He signals for BRIAN to keep quiet and begins to cautiously look around the room.*)

MARTY: (*Almost a whisper*) Did you see that? Sssh...Did you? Be as still as you can. I think the light's changing. You can't see it right away, 'cause it's tricky—you can't see it, but it's there. She's there.

BRIAN: Who's there?

MARTY: (*Still staring up at the mirror*) The woman in the mirror.

(*With his hand, MARTY reaches towards the ceiling mirror. Again, an illumination begins to emanate down towards him from the glass reflection——like a soft, radiant shine; it slowly begins to envelop him in its glow. But it's different from the last illumination; and it seems that not only can MARTY see it, but NATALIE sees it as well.*)

MARTY: (*Noticing her reaction*) You've seen her haven't you?

NATALIE: (*A beat*) Yes. I did.

MARTY: I knew it—I knew it! I could tell just by looking at you. If you don't mind my saying so, ma'am, you look a little spooked.

BRIAN: She always looks like that.

MARTY: *(To* BRIAN*)* Don't you believe in ghosts?

BRIAN: In a motel room in Manhattan? Of course not.

MARTY: What does location have to do with anything? You think ghosts can only be found in the country or in some castle in Europe? Ghosts are everywhere because people are everywhere.

NATALIE: I saw her.

MARTY: She showed herself to you.

NATALIE: Yes.

MARTY: *(Excitedly)* This is extraordinary! What did she look like? Do you remember what she looked like?

NATALIE: I remember her eyes.

MARTY: You didn't look directly into her eyes, did you? *(A beat)* Did you see them; did you see her eyes?

NATALIE: They were brown. They were brown and large and dark…I think she died in this room. I felt this sharp pain in the back of my neck

MARTY: Can you remember anything else?

BRIAN: *(To* NATALIE*)* Are you okay?

NATALIE: No. I think somebody broke her neck. *(She exits into bathroom)*

(A short beat as the two men stand for a moment, apparently unsure of what to do next. Then MARTY *takes out a small bottle of whiskey from an inside pocket in his jacket and waves it in front of* BRIAN. *He unwraps the plastic cups next to the coffeemaker and pours whiskey into both cups. He then hands* BRIAN *one of them.* BRIAN *seems a little reluctant.)*

BRIAN: I don't know.

MARTY: Come on…I bet it'll do you good.

BRIAN: *(Finally taking it)* Okay. What the hell…thanks.

MARTY: *(A beat)* Don't take this the wrong way, but that girl seems to be a jelly donut shy of a baker's dozen.

BRIAN: *(Laughs in spite of himself)* Actually, I would say that's a pretty fair assessment.

MARTY: *(Laughs as well)* I guess it would be pretty darn easy to get all tangled up in a lover's quarrel with her, right?

BRIAN: It wasn't a lover's quarrel.

MARTY: You like 'em wild, don't you?

BRIAN: She's unbalanced.

MARTY: *(Shrugs)* All women are fucking crazy.

BRIAN: No, I mean she's really unbalanced. *(Short beat)* She spent some time in the Psych Unit at Gracie Square Hospital.

MARTY: *(Eyes widen)* Oh!

BRIAN: I think it was a while ago, but still she…um… she has problems with depression… *(Almost to himself)* I should've known better.

MARTY: *(Laughs)* So, it's not that you like 'em wild, you just like 'em out of their fucking minds!

BRIAN: She seemed fine when I saw her last night. She was fine—

MARTY: *(Still laughing)* Oh, bro—I really feel for you, man…!

BRIAN: She was charming…warm…I don't understand what happened.

MARTY: I do… You weren't listening to the big noggin… *(Pointing to his crotch)* You were listening to the little one...! *(A short beat)* Either that or maybe you've got a bit of a 'death wish,' huh?

BRIAN: *(Smiles; nods)* Yeah, maybe. So what makes you such an authority on women?

MARTY: *(Shaking his head)* Oh, I'm not! Not at all. I just know what I know...my mother used to say that sex wasn't nearly as important as one's spirituality. She'd always tell me that instead of looking to get laid, I should be looking for a higher power.

BRIAN: That's good advice.

MARTY: I thought so. And when I was in high school, I'd masturbate on the roof of our house in Jersey every Sunday morning. I figured I was killing two birds with one stone there; I was getting off AND looking for my God in the heavens at the same time.

BRIAN: *(Laughs)* Sounds like a safe and commendable compromise.

MARTY: Yeah, and when my mother caught me, she almost lost her mind! *(Laughs; proudly)* I put that story in my play. My mother's in the play.

BRIAN: You're a writer?

MARTY: I am. And she's why I became a writer. It was because of my mother. She was a temp. She wanted to be an actress, but never got acting work, so she temped a lot. She was too old to wait on tables, but she could type pretty well and answer phones. I wanted to write plays for her. I wanted to give her the work that no one else would.

BRIAN: Where is she now? Still living in New Jersey?

MARTY: No.

(There is a long, uncomfortable beat as MARTY stares at BRIAN, unflinchingly. We can tell that BRIAN has begun

to feel a little uneasy by MARTY'S *direct gaze and he gulps down the rest of his drink.)*

BRIAN: *(Slight move towards the bathroom)* I should go check on Natalie.

MARTY: *(Hastily)* I'd love for you to read it.

BRIAN: Read what?

MARTY: Something of mine. Something I've written. Something I've been working on, actually.

BRIAN: *(After a short beat; hesitant)* I'd like to, Marty. I really would. But—

MARTY: But what?

BRIAN: *(Indicating the bathroom)* But first I'd have to figure out what to do with Natalie.

MARTY: *(Shrugs)* She's not your problem. She's a stray. It's all she is. You gave her what she wanted. She got to feel special for awhile. That's it. I used to bring home strays. It's a dangerous habit, I know. I feel sorry for them. They're completely at our mercy. They need so much. And we say we care, but only when it's convenient for us. We don't see that by showing them some attention, we give them a reason to exist. We don't care. Isn't that terrible?

BRIAN: *(Little defensive)* I know Natalie, alright? I've known her for years. We're friends.

MARTY: *(Pouring more whiskey in* BRIAN'S *cup)* Just 'cause you've known somebody for years don't mean you're friends, it just means you've known them for a long time. *(A short beat)* Natalie's got those big, hungry eyes...that desperate, struggling artist's smell about her...you can't miss it. My mother had the same smell. The same sticky-sweet, sweaty, tobacco, camphor powder-like smells...like the smell of an old man who's just swallowed a baby.

BRIAN: I never noticed that.

MARTY: *(Laughs)* That's 'cause you don't smell anything like that, man! Come on…you're like a brand-new, state-of-the-art air conditioner…! All nice and clean and fresh and cold, like snow and ice cubes and crunchy green leaves. It's like you're giving off your own fucking air. You're nothing like her… But you were fucking her, weren't you? The first time I came in…?

BRIAN: Well—

MARTY: The two of you were getting busy 'raw-dog,' right?
You were pumping Natalie.
See…that had to be exciting for her.
Having the chance to get pumped by a celebrity.
It's kind of a victory in itself, right?
It must have made her feel connected to what she longs for, huh? It must have made her feel accepted.

BRIAN: I don't know about that.

MARTY: *(Short beat)* Yes, you do, man.
You know it.
Your touch validates her.
It makes her real.
Suddenly…intensely real.
And isn't that a beautiful thing?
To be real?

BRIAN: *(After a beat)* She is real. Natalie is real.

MARTY: Well, there you go…your responsibility to her is over. *(Short beat; fierce whisper)* You know…I'd love to pump a famous person.

(BRIAN's not sure that he likes the sound of this, nor does he like the way MARTY is intensely staring at him again. A beat.)

BRIAN: *(Uneasy)* Marty…?

MARTY: *(Still staring at him; intense)* What?

BRIAN: I'm straight.

MARTY: *(Laughs)* Straight as a crow flies, right? *(A short beat)* I wanted to be a soldier once.

BRIAN: Really?

MARTY: Yeah.
Soldiers are HOT.
I mean a soldier gets slit, man.
A soldier gets about as much slit as a...well, as a celebrity...I guess...except I bet a celebrity can get a much higher caliber of sniz—
(Conspiratorial; leaning in) I mean, you do, right?
The good stuff.
The really glamorous gash.
Anytime you want it, right?
Oh man...I bet they're putting it in your face all the time, huh?
And not just the normal women either...not like her... not like Natalie...nah, fuck that—

BRIAN: Natalie is an attractive woman.

MARTY: Yeah, but she's normal, right?

BRIAN: What does that mean, "normal"?

MARTY: I mean, she's ordinarily attractive.
Of course, there's nothing wrong with that.
You can find girls like Natalie anywhere
But the kind of women I'm talking about
(In sudden rapture) Oh God...some of those women!
To see them up close
They must be...they must be...spectacular.
(Back to BRIAN; mischievous smile) And that's what you got, right?

I bet you've got your choice of that really tight, prime-twenty-something-year-old-nip-and-fuck-suck-botoxicating-L A—landing-strip-snatch, right?

(A beat. A slow, self-satisfied smile suddenly spreads across BRIAN'S *face as he faces* MARTY.)

BRIAN: Maybe.

*(*MARTY *gives out an exhilarated whoop and holler and hugs* BRIAN *in a brotherly, conspiratorial manner. Oddly enough, this becomes a lovely moment between the two men.* BRIAN *is smiling and seems suddenly more relaxed and warm towards* MARTY *in a way we have never saw him with* NATALIE.)

MARTY: Oh man! I knew it! I knew it! You are the *man*! My allegiance is *total* and beyond reproach. You are my fucking hero, you know that? My fucking hero!

BRIAN: *(Enjoying this)* Thank you, but I'm just an actor.

MARTY: *(Pouring him more whiskey)* All that pussy—

BRIAN: *(Last stab at modesty; indicating they should keep their voices down)* Well, in theory, of course...!

MARTY: Fuck theory, I'm talking about reality, baby! REAL pussy as opposed to the theoretical kind... *(Thinks a moment; relishing his thoughts)* ...Hey...you know...that's a good name for a band—Theoretical Pussy...!

*(*MARTY *and* BRIAN *find this amusing as well and continue to laugh and enjoy the moment.)*

MARTY: *(Eager)* Can I tell you about my play now?

*(*BRIAN *suddenly seems deflated by the question. He sighs.)*

BRIAN: Look, Marty...like I told you before, I'd love to...but—

MARTY: But?

BRIAN: But I need to make sure Natalie's okay.

(MARTY *stares at him for a moment, walks over to the bathroom, and knocks firmly on the door.*)

BRIAN: (*To* MARTY) Hey don't do that...she might not be...finished...

(NATALIE *enters from the bathroom.*)

NATALIE: I need a cigarette.

BRIAN: What's wrong?

NATALIE: I think it happened again. While I was on the toilet, I heard her. She was asking me questions.

MARTY: The woman in the mirror?

NATALIE: Yes.

MARTY: Are you sure?

NATALIE: (*Sarcasm*) I don't normally just hear voices from out of nowhere, okay?

MARTY: (*Almost to himself*) Well, that's not what I hear—

BRIAN: (*Signaling him*) Marty—don't...

(*This stops* NATALIE, *who immediately looks towards* BRIAN, *accusingly.*)

NATALIE: Did you tell him? You fucking told him, didn't you?

BRIAN: Natalie—

NATALIE: You told him about Gracie Square, didn't you?

BRIAN: I may have mentioned it...very briefly...

MARTY: It's nothing to be ashamed of, miss.

NATALIE: (*Defensive*) I'm not crazy, okay?

MARTY: (*Slightly patronizing*) Well, of course you're not. And even if you were...that's okay, too. I once

had a cousin who was convinced she was Eleanor of
Aquitaine.

NATALIE: You know…I thought I heard laughter. The
two of you have been laughing at me, haven't you?

BRIAN: No. Not at all.

MARTY: *(An attempt to be helpful)* No, we really want to
hear more about the voices in your head.

BRIAN: Marty!

NATALIE: Fuck you both.

MARTY: It's just that all the sightings of the woman
have taken place here. Not in the bathroom. Right here,
in this room.

NATALIE: I didn't say I *saw* her—I said that I heard
her! She asked if I was an actress. I said I used to be,
but that I was a playwright now. And she said she'd
always wanted to be in the theatre because it's so
glamorous… She said she'd never spend the rest of her
life working as some nobody in an office. She knew she
was special.

*(The light bulb stutters. They all notice this. NATALIE walks
over to the window.)*

NATALIE: She said she was outside.
She was dangling out there…in the street…upside
down.
And she told me she was taken and carried to the
motel,
Away from the collapsed building, away from the site,
away from the streets, from everyone else…and she
was brought into this room.

*(NATALIE grabs her bag, taking out her pack of cigarettes
and a lighter. She moves towards the door.)*

BRIAN: Nat…?

(NATALIE *doesn't answer and quickly rushes out. A beat.* BRIAN *faces* MARTY *almost angrily.*)

BRIAN: Did you have to do that? Did you have to let her know I told you?

MARTY: (*Sheepish*) I'm…I'm sorry; man…it just came out. I wasn't thinking.

BRIAN: (*After a short beat*) Should I go after her?

MARTY: No. I'm sure she's just gone for a smoke. She'll be back. Her coat's still here.

(*Another beat as* BRIAN *continues to look towards where* NATALIE *has exited. Then he sighs deeply, almost in a resigned manner. He sits down on the edge of the bed facing* MARTY.)

BRIAN: Okay then…why don't you tell me about your play?

MARTY: (*A short beat*) Are you serious?

BRIAN: Well, I can't leave without Natalie, and she's been jonesing for a smoke since we got here…

MARTY: (*Excitedly*) Oh man—

BRIAN: …So I figure you might as well tell me about your play while we wait.

MARTY: (*Thrilled*) Oh man! This is great. Thank you. Thank you so much. (*He takes a moment to "prepare" himself*) Well…I can't start without mentioning my inspiration for it first.

BRIAN: Okay.

MARTY: (*Almost proudly*) It's this room.
Oh, this room…! This room has been the REAL inspiration.
It's been my muse.
I know muses are supposed to be women.

And in a way, the woman in the mirror is a muse of sorts.
But it's the room that got me going.
Light bulbs flickering on and off.
That hideous little flies' nest at the window...the humming of a busted radiator, the bleachy-sweat smell of Lysol
The feel and sense of dust kitties—
You know, when they found the woman's body in here
They had no idea where it came from
Can you imagine?
Oh Man...what a gorgeous mystery...!
And you know how people are—they take shit for granted all the time.
They just assumed she was brought in from the accident outside
That's what was said in the newspapers anyway
A reporter assumed that some sick creep found her body and brought it in here for a little necro-fellatio; you know what I'm saying?
I mean...that's how urban legends get started, right?
It's not about the accident. That part's normal.
Accidents happen in the city all the time...all the fucking time...buildings fall down, cranes collapse, manhole covers explode, subways get evacuated...
that's not the part that's scary...hell no...it's the idea...
the idea that from one seemingly almost normal, isolated incident...something really awful...really creepy, and just downright horrifying...can end up coming out of it.
But hey! I'm getting ahead of myself here—
(With a slight flourish)
The play begins...
The opening scene takes place in a room just like this one.

Just a plain, little motel room
And this room is in the kind of motel that men and
women will come to
From time to time.
When they think no one's looking.
When they're just thinking of getting away for a little
something-something, you know…for a little bit of
strange.
They come here for privacy.
But there's a problem
There's a problem with the room they're in
It's haunted
And they know this because the security guard
(He's the protagonist, by the way.)
The security guard who works at the motel barges in
on them
And he tells them a story
A ghost story
The ghost, he tells them, is a woman
A beautiful woman
He says her face appears now and again
Glowing in the ceiling mirror that hovers right above
the bed
The woman died on the day of the accident, the day
the building collapsed, he tells the couple
Like so many of those other poor people out there.
The protagonist goes on to tell them how he drove his
mother to work that morning.
She's a temp, you see, and she has an assignment that
day
It's also right across the street from the motel.
And she runs out of the car.
He doesn't understand why she does this
It seems such a nutty, thoughtless thing to do

He thinks that maybe she's running to go help
someone, but he's not sure.

And he runs after her.

He doesn't know what he's running into...he just has to
find her.

But it's chaos...all white, paper, rock and granite
CHAOS...you think there's anybody at the motel once
the building collapses? At that moment, there's only
one place for people to be... *(Pointing towards window)*
Right out there—on the streets.

And there are people everywhere; all of them, up
against and all around him like some hot, boiling
swarm.

He runs into someplace where the sprinklers must
have gone cockeyed 'cause suddenly there's water
everywhere

The water fills his shoes like a corroded tank that
overflows.

And he realizes that he's not outside anymore. Now,
he's all alone, and running down a long dark hallway,
with what looks like a smooth, Italian marble floor.

The black veins in the flooring seem to shimmer
against the water, like blue cheese covered in ice.

And his shoes are completely soaked; they clack noisily
against the limestone.

(Short beat) But off to his right, he sees a giant wall
completely made of glass.

And that's when he sees her.

She's on the other side of the glass—

BRIAN: His mother...

MARTY: No. Not his mother.

She's hanging upside down—

BRIAN: The woman...

MARTY: Yes. He has to take her down. She has to be taken down from there, doesn't she?

BRIAN: Does he call for help?

MARTY: Who's he supposed to call? She's nobody. She probably temps in an office, too. She's probably an artist... just like you and me.
She's just...stuck there...hanging from a girder
Hanging by her jacket
The girder's angled
And she's just hanging there
Upside down.
Her jacket's all tangled up with the metal
So he knows he has to use his pocket-knife to cut it off...to bring her down...to take hold of her.
And once he takes her down...that's it. She's his. She belongs to him.

BRIAN: (*A short beat*) I don't understand. He just 'took' her?

MARTY: Oh, people can be taken.
(*A beat*) It's tricky...very tricky...you have to make sure you don't get caught
Then, you have to make sure nobody's watching
That nobody will disturb you
And that you'll have the privacy you need
To do...whatever it is...you deem necessary
At that moment—
But people can be taken
You can *take* anybody you want
And whoever she was...she was nothing; she didn't even exist. I mean, when you think about it—by taking her, he's giving her a life. Because at that moment, she's the most important thing in the world to him—

(MARTY *looks at* BRIAN. *A beat*)

MARTY: You don't like it.

BRIAN: It's not that.

MARTY: There's more.

BRIAN: I really can't give you any kind of appraisal without reading the script first.

MARTY: But you can let me finish my story. You can do that, can't you? Can't you? You can let me finish my story, and then you can tell me what you think. What you really think.

BRIAN: You should take my card. This way you can send it to me later—

MARTY: But what do you think of it so far? Could you at least tell me that?

BRIAN: Well…it's…it's certainly…interesting. It…it just…it does seem a little complicated for the stage…I mean, with all the running around your protagonist is doing, you might want to consider turning this into a screenplay instead…and also, I'm concerned that the whole 'ghost' situation may come across as a bit banal—

MARTY: B-banal?

BRIAN: Most people know that ghosts don't actually exist.

MARTY: But this room is haunted. You believe that, don't you?

BRIAN: (Slightly patronizing) Well, I know you believe it, Marty…and I respect your opinion…but I've been here just as long as Natalie has and I haven't seen anything.

MARTY: But Natalie saw her.

BRIAN: Natalie has her own issues.

(BRIAN's cell phone rings. He checks to see who it is. He turns towards MARTY.)

BRIAN: I'm sorry, I have to take this. *(Into phone)* Hey man, how's it going? Listen, I can't talk now; call me back in a bit. Yeah, like in twenty minutes? *(A beat; laughs low)* Oh man...just wait...just fucking wait... yeah... *(Laughs again)* Okay, man...soon...talk soon.

(MARTY hears all this and we see how it affects him. BRIAN shuts off the phone. By this time, MARTY has taken out his collapsible baton from his waist belt and hits BRIAN across the head. BRIAN stands, stunned for a moment, his cell phone falls to the floor. MARTY hits him again. And again. And again. And again. BRIAN'S body crumbles to the side of the bed. MARTY stands for a moment. NATALIE enters. She sees the body and gasps. A dramatic beat.)

MARTY: This was stupid.

NATALIE: Is he dead?

MARTY: This was so stupid.

NATALIE: *(Checks BRIAN'S body)* Oh... Fuck, Marty—

MARTY: I should never have listened to you.

NATALIE: I don't understand...why? Why did you do this? It was going well—

MARTY: He didn't let me finish.

NATALIE: What?

MARTY: I didn't finish. He wouldn't let me finish my fucking story.

NATALIE: Then you convince him to let you finish... you don't kill him.

MARTY: He laughed at me. The patronizing son of a bitch. The fucking, prick asshole. I heard him laughing at me over the phone.

NATALIE: Oh my God—how do you know that? How do you know he was laughing at you?

MARTY: I could tell.

NATALIE: Bullshit.

MARTY: You went too far.

NATALIE: How?

MARTY: You went too far.

NATALIE: I did what we agreed on.

MARTY: Too fucking far!

NATALIE: I can't believe this. I cannot fucking believe you did this. You said you could handle it. That you could do it.

MARTY: I can do it. I can do things.

NATALIE: All you needed to do was be his friend. Get him on your side—

MARTY: I did that.

NATALIE: You were supposed to make him like you.

MARTY: He did. He was starting to like me a lot, I could tell.

NATALIE: And then once he's comfortable with you, you tell him all about the play we wrote, remember?

MARTY: I know—I know! I did that. I did all of it.

NATALIE: And once you told him about the play, he'd be impressed enough to introduce you to Spencer. And then Spencer produces it with Brian playing the lead. That's it. That's *all* you needed to do.

MARTY: I know…

NATALIE: And you said you could do it…!

MARTY: I know! (*A little helplessly; a short beat*) But he didn't like it.

NATALIE: Didn't like what?

MARTY: The play…he didn't like our play.

NATALIE: Did he tell you that?

MARTY: *(Almost afraid to say it)* N-No.

NATALIE: *(At wit's end; shouting)* THEN HOW DID YOU KNOW HE DIDN'T LIKE IT?

(A beat. MARTY *attempts to say something, but is unable. He can only weakly motion towards her with his hands. The gesture is almost comic in its plainness. He even looks as though he may burst into tears. With some effort,* NATALIE *takes a long moment to calm herself down. With one more glance towards* BRIAN'S *prone body, she sits at the edge of the bed.)*

NATALIE: It's okay. I'm sorry…I'm sorry, baby…maybe you're right. Maybe this was all…too much.
Just too much.
(Short beat) When we saw each other at that staged reading,
Brian and I…I could tell…I could see it in his eyes…
What he wanted…what he wanted from me.
He's never taken me seriously as an artist,
But that's only because I haven't had the opportunities he's had
I haven't known… *(With some bitterness)*…the right people. Like he has.
But I knew…I knew that he's always had a thing for me.
And it made me feel good.
Knowing that someone like him wanted to fuck me.
I don't know…it…it gave me power.
And most of the time…
I don't feel particularly powerful in this world, you know?
And I thought…hey; why not take advantage of that?
Why not use it to help me? To help us?
So I flirted with him… I told him my troubles and
I put on the waterworks, I orated lovely, flattering

words, shook myself silly, crossed my legs, fluttered
my lashes, I made him 'buy it', made him want to do
things, like hold me, comfort me, tell me it's all going
to be all right, tell me he wants to help, tell me I'm a
peach, a dream, a 'nice' girl underneath all the make-
up and the uncertainty...But the whole time I was
lying through my goddamn teeth and I was doing it *for
us.*

MARTY: Natalie...

NATALIE: I brought Brian here so you could tell him
about the play we wrote together.

MARTY: I know that.

NATALIE: And we were up until five this morning
working out all the details...every single detail...what
time we would get here, when you would be knocking
on the door, so we could let you in, and then you could
meet him...

MARTY: *(Nodding)* It was a good plan.

NATALIE: Brian knew I was married, of course, but he's
never *met* you, he didn't know anything about you, so
he'd have no way of knowing that you worked here as
a security guard—

MARTY: It almost worked.

NATALIE: And now...everything's been blown. *(Short
beat)* Do you understand that, baby? Do you get that?
Brian's dead...Spencer's gone...

MARTY: We still have Spencer.

NATALIE: No, no, baby...not without Brian—we don't
have shit without Brian.

MARTY: But look...I have Brian's phone now. He's got
Spencer's number on speed dial, right?

NATALIE: Oh, and what? We call Spencer and say,
"Hi, we're a couple of playwrights and we just wrote

a play, which we'd love for you to read and consider producing...What's that? How did we get your number? Oh, well, we killed your friend Brian and stole his phone. Would you like to read the play before we get put in jail for the rest of *our fucking lives*?"

MARTY: *(A beat)* You call Spencer and tell him you wrote the play.

NATALIE: No—

MARTY: You tell him you're a friend of Brian's and you have a play to give him.

NATALIE: Baby, please...

MARTY: I'll turn myself in. And you'll give Spencer the play and tell him you wrote it.

NATALIE: You're not going to jail.

MARTY: I have to—

NATALIE: No. *(Beat; thinking quickly)* We'll get rid of the body. We'll get rid of it.

MARTY: How? How do we do that?

(Suddenly alert, NATALIE *stands up.)*

NATALIE: Help me get him into the bathroom.

MARTY: What good will that do?

NATALIE: I don't know! Marty, for God's sakes, help me carry him—

MARTY: *(Blocks her; his manner suddenly violent)* Don't touch him!

NATALIE: It's okay. I just need to put him in the bathroom.

MARTY: No. I don't want you touching him anymore.

*(*NATALIE *looks at* MARTY *and sees for the first time that he's out of it. She realizes something. By this time, she's begun scratching her arm; this appears to be a nervous tic.)*

NATALIE: When did you stop taking your meds?

MARTY: I'm taking yours.

NATALIE: *(Scratching continues)* You can't do that, baby. Not with your blood pressure.

MARTY: I can't take mine any longer. They were making me see the walls breathe.

NATALIE: Walls don't breathe.

MARTY: Not when you're looking. They wait until you're asleep, or you're reading or watching TV—then they slowly begin to follow the rhythm of your own breathing—

NATALIE: *(Scratching is getting worse)* No, no...they don't, baby. They really don't do that at all.

MARTY: I see them do it. I see those walls. I look up...at the ceiling...

(MARTY looks up, seeing the mirror. He stops and notices NATALIE scratching. He goes over to her.)

MARTY: *(This bothers him)* Stop that.

NATALIE: What?

MARTY: Please...please stop doing that. It looks like you're trying to tear the skin off your arm 'cause there're hundreds of tiny ants underneath.

NATALIE: Oh God, Marty—

MARTY: And those ants will find some way...some opening through your skin...through the membrane... to get out...and if you keep scratching it like that, your nails will tear a huge hole right into your skin and all the ants will come bursting out, swimming through the blood and the water and pus, and then there'll be ants all over the floor and the room, and we won't be able to get house-cleaning to clean it up 'cause they'll be afraid of infection and then those cocksuckers in management will tell me that I have to clean up all the ants by myself.

NATALIE: Okay. It's okay. There are no ants. See? No ants here at all.

MARTY: Are you angry with me?

NATALIE: You're my God, aren't you? You are my God.

(A beat. MARTY visibly relaxes and chuckles.)

MARTY: I'm not, actually. He's in the subway.

NATALIE: Who is?

MARTY: God.

NATALIE: *(Attempt at a smile)* Oh, really?

MARTY: That's right. There's a guy on the F train who walks up and down the subway car holding a trapper keeper in front of his face. As soon as the doors close, he announces to everyone in the car that he's God.

NATALIE: That's not very original. There were at least seven Gods at Gracie Square.

MARTY: *(Brightening; a happy memory)* Gracie Square! Oh man, if those jerks could see us now, huh?

NATALIE: I'm glad they can't.

MARTY: I wish they could've seen you, baby. I wish all those fuckers from Gracie Square could've seen you today. You were amazing.

NATALIE: When?

MARTY: *(Proudly)* The way you kept talking about the woman in the mirror. You did it with such intensity.

NATALIE: You're not too bad yourself. But what was all that bullshit before about the smoking?

MARTY: There's no smoking in the building.

NATALIE: Then why didn't you just say that?

MARTY: (Shrugs) You wanted to look bad in front of Brian. You said it would make him warm up to me more easily.

NATALIE: You made me look stupid.

MARTY: (He holds her; adoringly) You can never be stupid. You're my goddess.

NATALIE: (Imitating him) "Who's Ernest Borgnine?"

(A sudden flash of mirth between MARTY and NATALIE. Seems to be an "inside" joke.)

MARTY: (A little sheepish) Okay. Maybe I overdid it a little with the "Jersey rube" act—

NATALIE: (Smile) Maybe just a little.

MARTY: But not you. You were incredible. You really had Brian spooked. You're such a great actress.

NATALIE: Actually, I spooked myself.

MARTY: How?

NATALIE: I think I started to believe it.

(MARTY laughs.)

NATALIE: I really thought I saw a face.

MARTY: Who needs their meds now?

NATALIE: I'm serious. The way we kept talking about it...it made me almost start to believe the story and I think I started seeing things. And then, that strange light bulb and being in this room the whole time! (Almost a pleasant memory) Oh...it was perfect. Just perfect.

MARTY: I told you...the room was my inspiration. When they found the woman's body in here, they just assumed she was brought in right from the accident, but nobody really knows what happened. Nobody knows for sure.

NATALIE: *(Nodding; proudly)* It should have worked beautifully. We put Brian right into the heart of the story.

MARTY: *(Thinking about it; chuckles)* Yeah…and now he *is* the story.

NATALIE: Oh my God… *(Covers her mouth with a muffled laugh)* Do you think he'll start haunting the room? That would be so weird…! If it wasn't haunted before it sure as shit is now, right?

MARTY: I don't think he'd haunt strangers…unless of course, he wants them to ask for an autograph.

NATALIE: *(Short beat)* No. It won't be the room that he haunts; it'll be me.

MARTY: Why do you say that?

NATALIE: We could leave the body here and go, but he'll follow me.

MARTY: No. He can't hurt you.

NATALIE: We have to get rid of it.

MARTY: When the housekeeper comes in tomorrow morning, we'll already be long gone.

NATALIE: I'm going to take his eyes.

MARTY: Don't say disgusting things.

NATALIE: That way he won't be able to see me—I won't have to feel him staring at me.

MARTY: I don't want his eyes in my house.

NATALIE: We'll keep them in the freezer. That way you won't see them.

MARTY: But I'll know they're there. And every time I go to fetch a Popsicle, I'll have to bypass his fucking eyes.

NATALIE: *(She has a plan)* First we have to take him out of the room in pieces.

MARTY: *(Horrified by the idea)* Jesus, Natalie—that will make such a mess...!

NATALIE: That's why we have to put him in the bathroom first. If we can keep everything in the bathroom, it'll be that much easier to clean up. We'll need a few things—

MARTY: We can't. We can't do this. Not without being seen.

NATALIE: Who's going to see us? The housekeepers?

MARTY: *(Checks his watch)* They've left for the day.

NATALIE: Who else is here?

MARTY: The front desk clerk and the day manager. The night manager comes in about an hour. His office is downstairs next to the lobby. He hardly ever comes up here.

NATALIE: And how many rooms are occupied right now?

MARTY: Only six. It's been a slow day.

NATALIE: *(This is all a plus)* That's great. Then we have all night. We can do this, Marty. There's a place on Mott Street called Kam Kuo where you can buy those really big, thick-handled cleavers—the dexter carbon steel kind— *(By this time, she already has gone to her bag and taken out her organizer and a pen; she methodically begins making a list.)*

MARTY: No. No cutting.

NATALIE: The ones that come with the slightly serrated blades that get sharper as you keep using it. We're going to need a couple of those. Also, we need plastic sheeting—*lots* of plastic sheeting. I know they sell it in long rolls at Home Depot.

MARTY: *(This upsets him)* Shut-up Natalie...

NATALIE: *(She's on a roll)* You should probably get at least fifteen to twenty rolls. And while you're there, we'll need extra large, industrial strength pliers for his teeth as well as bolt cutters for his fingers.

MARTY: What the hell for?

NATALIE: We're going to use the pliers to take all his teeth out. And the bolt cutters will remove the tips of his fingers. So, they can't identify his body. Oh! And don't forget we'll need big, black, plastic bags. But not the heavy-duty Hefty bags you find at the supermarket; those aren't strong enough...I'm talking about the contractor bags, the ones that won't tear easily, the ones you find on the construction sites...!

MARTY: I can't go and get all that stuff now—

NATALIE: Of course you can, we need it.

MARTY: *(A mix of stubbornness and disgust)* No, we don't. It's too much work.

NATALIE: And we'll need fresh clothes. We'll have to burn these since they'll be covered with blood. You'll have to stop by our place first and get clothes for the two of us. I got your spare uniform from the cleaners yesterday; it's hanging in the closet, so make sure you bring it with you. And try to bring me clothes that look as close as possible to what I'm already wearing. That way, I won't look so different when I leave the motel.

MARTY: Natalie, I can't do this. It's too much...!

NATALIE: Yes, there'll be a lot of stuff, but you'll just bring it in a little bit at a time...that way the manager and the front desk clerk won't get suspicious. It'll be fine, Marty; we have all night.

MARTY: Why can't we roll the body up in a long rug and carry it out of the motel later tonight? We're close enough to the river that we could just dump the whole thing in the water.

NATALIE: It's okay, baby, we are going to dump it in the water. But there are things we have to do first. You can't worry about the extra work. This isn't the time for laziness. We have to think now.

MARTY: I am thinking. Don't talk to me like I'm an idiot.

NATALIE: I'm not. I don't think you're an idiot.

MARTY: You're coming with me; this is too much shit to carry.

NATALIE: I can't. I have to stay here with Brian.

(This is the wrong thing to say. This stops MARTY. A beat. He stares at NATALIE.)

MARTY: You want to stay with him?

NATALIE: Do you want to leave the body here alone? Do you really want to take that chance?

MARTY: I won't leave you here with him.

NATALIE: Somebody has to stay.

MARTY: (Anger mounting) Why the fuck does it have to be you?

NATALIE: Marty—

MARTY: Haven't you spent enough time with him already? Or do you need more? Do you still need more time in his exalted fucking presence?

NATALIE: This isn't about that. This is about us.

MARTY: Us? Oh, this is about us!

NATALIE: It's always been about us—

MARTY: Oh, I see…that's very funny; I can't believe I missed that. We're you thinking about US when he had his prick inside you?

NATALIE: Marty, come on. Help me take his clothes off.

MARTY: *(Blocking her)* DON'T TOUCH HIM.

NATALIE: Marty, please—

MARTY: I mean it; you keep away from him. Your hands have been covered enough with him; they're covered with his spooge—

NATALIE: We have to deal with his body!

MARTY: You've dealt with it enough! *(Short beat)* Did you fuck Brian before I knocked on the door?

NATALIE: You promised you wouldn't ask me about that.

MARTY: *(Livid)* I know you did.
Don't lie to me, Natalie...don't you *dare* fucking lie to me because I know you did.
And you liked it. *(A beat)* I could tell you liked it.
When I walked in here, I could smell the room and I knew.
I saw your face and I knew.
Your fucking face.
It gives you away, you know—that fucking, lying face of yours.
You're such a good, fucking actress, aren't you?
(Short beat) I said it can go in your mouth.
Didn't I say that?
I said oh yes, Natalie, indeed Natalie, if it comes to that,
If there's a chance of our blowing it, then you blow the dick.
You go right ahead.
If it's totally necessary, and the dick absolutely...
positively must be attended to in some way,
In some immediate fashion, then yes, by all means...let it go in your mouth.

I will make allowances.
I will *accept* what needs to be acknowledged.
I won't be a bastard over a little oral-tug-and-suck;
I will not be a complete prude.
I'll allow for it, but nothing more—nothing more—no
further fucking orifices allowed!

NATALIE: It all went faster than I expected.

MARTY: Too fast for a signal? You never gave me the
signal. I was out in the hallway, waiting, and you never
sent it. I had to make up the story about the wallet just
to get in here.

NATALIE: I know. I know. I'm sorry.

MARTY: You're sorry? Sorry for what? Sorry that he's
dead? Maybe you secretly wanted him. Maybe you
even loved him. Maybe this was never about getting
the play to Brian. Maybe this had nothing to do with
Spencer producing our play. Maybe it was only about
FUCKING Brian. That's all you really wanted—just
to be a little star-fucker. Is that what you are? Is that
what I'm married to? Just a little star-fucker? A LITTLE
STAR-FUCKER ALL SET TO FUCK THAT FUCKING
FUCKER!

NATALIE: Shut up.

MARTY: Say it; "I'm a little star-fucker!"

NATALIE: NO!

MARTY: *(To the tune of "I'm A Little Teapot")*
I'm a little star-fucker
Immoral and blunt
Here are my titties
And here's my dirty cunt…!

NATALIE: *(She's had it)* Go ahead, sing…sing your
fucking songs, YOU SICK WEIRDO! Let everyone in
the building know what you've done; how you fucked

this up! How you fucked it for us! Holler until they hear you out in the street.

MARTY: You are a never-was, no-talent, hairy fuck-monster without a soul.

NATALIE: Yes, that's it. Louder. Say it louder.

MARTY: Don't tell me what to do.

NATALIE: Oh, no...you already know what to do, don't you? Don't you? When they come to arrest you, you can tell them how close we got, how it almost worked—how I was the one who covered every angle—

MARTY: The play was MY inspiration. You don't know what it means to be inspired; you're only inspired by the nasty twitch between your legs.

NATALIE: I got him for you. I *gave* him to you on a silver plate and then you fucked up the very last chance I had. You *broke* my plate.

MARTY: I did not!

NATALIE: You *smashed* my plate into a thousand little mirrors...seven years of shit luck for each mirror multiplied into a thousand. That's what you gave me.

MARTY: I didn't. I *never* touched your fucking plate.

NATALIE: You think that surprises me?
Nothing you do surprises me, Marty.
You are *beyond* surprises.
You can't even be trusted to take out the fucking garbage!
I always have to remind you... "No, Marty; the garbage gets picked up only on Tuesday and Thursday mornings. The truck comes only on Tuesday and Thursday mornings!

MARTY: I've gotten better about that, you fucking bitch. You don't give me credit.

NATALIE: I can't help it! I have high standards...!
I don't give credit for unfinished work.

MARTY: I finish what I start. I'm a security guard. You
don't get to be a security guard without being able to
handle responsibility. I work every day at this fucking
motel, supporting you. I see the day through—I see it, I
accept it, and I finish it.

NATALIE: You never finished the story.

MARTY: *(Almost an agonized wail)* I wasn't allowed to
finish!

NATALIE: Allowed? You need to be allowed to do
things? What are you, a child? Am I your mother?
Are you a little baby, Marty? Have I been married to a
fucking useless baby this whole time?
I thought you were a man.
A man doesn't worry about being capable. He doesn't
wait to be 'allowed.'
Only a child waits.
Only a child hesitates.
Only a child worries about being capable.
And you are *incapable*.
You are incompetent, Marty. Powerless. Inept.
A fucking mama's boy!
A clumsy, ham-fisted joke of a man.
You are a piece of corn riddled shit that hits the
proverbial fan *once*, and then for some reason, just
keeps hitting it over and over and over and over
again...!

*(MARTY grabs NATALIE and begins to choke her. He
squeezes her neck with a terrible force. NATALIE struggles
in his grasp, trying to call his name out, her arms flailing,
and at times managing to land a few blows upon his head,
shoulders, and arms. MARTY makes "Ssshing" sounds to
her, but continues to squeeze and press his fingers ever more*

tightly. She's losing strength; she closes her eyes. Her body slumps against the bed. A long beat. MARTY *stares at her for a moment, and then lets her go.*)

MARTY: *(Short beat; he returns to the 'story')* He didn't hear any breathing.
When he carried the woman off the street
He heard NOTHING.
I mean, she fell out of a fucking building!
Who's going to survive that?
Through the window blinds, the flurry of paper, through all the glass!
All the debris that must've passed through her
Settling itself into her beautiful, cold body
Into her skin.
How could she still be alive?
And then he heard something...
He had to lean in
He leaned in so closely
Right into her chest
That he almost missed it
And there it was—
Her heartbeat.

(Sounds of a heartbeat. MARTY *hears it, and we can see that it catches him off guard. He hastily moves away from* NATALIE's *body on the bed. He is reliving the moment. The pulsing sounds of the heartbeat rises.)*

MARTY: Oh, no, no, no, NO...!
Her heartbeat's getting stronger
It's getting louder
She's alive
This is not *good*!
He couldn't go back outside.
He couldn't let anyone know he took her.
He didn't know what to do.

Then suddenly, the woman opened her eyes
And she spoke to him
But her voice…it wasn't clear…it wasn't lucid.
It almost didn't sound human.
It was…burbly
She told him she was in pain. So much pain.
And she asked him if he would help her.
But he did nothing. Nothing.
After all, she was only a stray.
She needed to understand that.
She needed to realize that in the larger scheme of
things…
She didn't matter much.
And he watched her until she stopped talking.
Until she stopped pleading. Until she was motionless.
And quiet. *(A beat)* He saw the light then. Growing
from her still body
To him, it looked almost like a vapor
A vibrant, mounting steam rising up from her body
Swelling up towards the ceiling, up into the mirror.
Blending like creamy amber smoke deep within the
glass.
And that's when he knew.
Her spirit would always be trapped inside the mirror.

(A beat. The clock radio goes on by itself. MARTY *is startled
by this and turns it off. The light bulb stutters.* MARTY
*senses something; he turns his head and sees the face of the
woman in the mirror. Her face is terrible, almost grimacing.
Lights change. Suddenly, she is right there in the room with
all of them.* MARTY *cries out in fear, and clutches wildly
at his chest. The woman reaches her arm out towards him.
Lights change again and the woman disappears. Another
quiet beat.* NATALIE *takes a sharp intake of breath, most
likely coughing and sputtering. She sits up abruptly,
clutching her throat, and sees* MARTY, *a miserable slump*

on the floor. Another beat, as she slowly moves off the bed;
highly agitated and uncertain, as she fretfully looks to
MARTY'S *body and then towards* BRIAN'S *body. She looks*
up towards the ceiling mirror... Suddenly, BRIAN'S *cell*
phone, still on the floor, begins to ring. NATALIE *stares at*
the phone. She then timidly picks it up.)

NATALIE: *(Answering it)* Hello?
Oh. Spencer. Yes.
This is Natalie.
I'm a friend of Brian's.
Oh, I'm fine. How are you?
No. Brian...Brian's in the bathroom
But he wished for the two of us to meet.
I've written a play that he wants you to take a look at.
Yes. I'd be happy to meet you for a drink.
Yes. I did.
I wrote it.
(A beat) I'm a playwright.

(Outside the window, the buzzing from the flies rapidly
escalates until it appears that a starburst blast has taken
place, flooding the room in its radiance. A barrage flashes of
light sparkle the stage. The light bulb begins to flicker on and
off. NATALIE *stares at the light bulb sputtering vigorously*
until it finally goes out, leaving the stage in darkness.)

END OF PLAY